SCHIRMER'S LIBRAR
OF MUSICAL CLASSICS

Vol. 42

JOHN FIELD

Eighteen Nocturnes

For the Piano

Revised by
FRANZ LISZT

With an Essay by
FRANZ LISZT

and

A Biographical Sketch of the Author by
DR. THEODORE BAKER

G. SCHIRMER, *Inc.*

DISTRIBUTED BY

HAL•LEONARD™
CORPORATION

7777 W. BLUEMOUND RD. P.O. BOX 13819 MILWAUKEE, WI 53213

THE subject of this sketch was born in Dublin on July 26, 1782, and came of a musical family, his father being a violinist in a Dublin theatre, while his grandfather, who was an organist, gave him his first instruction in musical theory and piano-playing. His musical training was conducted with such extreme severity, on the part of both his father and grandfather, that young Field once (according to Fetis) fairly ran away from home, though utter destitution soon forced him to return. There can be no doubt that this undue severity and his enforced

application to study had a baneful influence on both his character and constitution; weakening the latter, which was never robust, and fostering a natural tendency to shy melancholy which developed into the careless indifference and apathy of his later years. His father obtaining an engagement at Bath, England, and thereafter at the Haymarket Theatre in London, the boy was brought to the latter city, and subsequently apprenticed (for a premium of 100 guineas) to Clementi, then in the full tide of success as a conductor, performer, teacher, and man of business. Young Field served for years in his master's salesrooms as a salesman showing off the pianos to customers; Up to the year 1804 he also had regular lessons from Clementi in piano-playing; in 1802 he accompanied him to Paris, where he created a genuine sensation in the musical world by his wonderful interpretation of Bach's and Handel's fugues. Clementi, however, was too much of a business man to give up the services of so valuable a salesman, and still kept him at his old employment of showing off pianos. From Paris they proceeded later to Germany and Russia; at St. Petersburg Field met Spohr, who gives a highly interesting description of him in his Autobiography. He was then to be found in Clementi's warerooms, "a pale, melancholy youth, awkward and shy, speaking no language but his own, and in clothes which he had far outgrown; but he had only to place his hands on the keys for all such drawbacks to be forgotten."

Clementi left St. Petersburg in 1804, but Field settled there permanently as a teacher and virtuoso, and attained extraordinary popularity in both capacities. On a concert tour to Moscow, undertaken in 1823, he met with even more brilliant success as a pianist than in the rival capital. He played in various other Russian towns, and in 1832 again appeared in London, where he gave a concert at the Philharmonic, playing a concerto of his own composition. Hence he proceeded to Paris, and in the following year to Italy, passing through Belgium and Switzerland on his way thither; but in Milan, Venice, and Naples his playing disappointed his aristocratic audiences, who had anticipated a brilliant display of pianoforte pyrotechnics, and felt no sympathy for the pale, unimpassioned pianist with the soft, dreamy touch and exuberance of melancholy. His concerts did not pay expenses; and worse, a combination of physical disorders which had been growing upon him for years now seized on and

utterly prostrated him. For nine long months Field lay in a hospital at Naples; he was rescued at length, though in a most wretched plight, by a Russian family named Raemanow, on condition that he should return with them to Moscow. Passing through Vienna on the way, his exquisite performance of his Nocturnes gained him enthusiastic applause; but this success was only transient—his powers were fast waning. During his last years complete indifference took possession of him, influencing all his personal habits; to rise, to sit down again, to walk, was fatiguing to him. A light cane was at times too heavy a burden for his indolent hand, and if he let it drop from sheer lack of energy to hold it, he would remain standing beside it till some passer-by picked it up for him. He died in Moscow January 11, 1837.

Field's execution was distinguished for taste and exquisite delicacy, and characterized by an extreme ease and placidity of manner which sometimes amounted to a morbid languor and indifference. To avoid all unnecessary agitation it was his habit to place a coin on the back of his hand, and to practise his daily exercises for hours with it in that position. His touch was smooth and even, and the legato perfect, with a loose wrist and entire absence of exertion; the tone suave and singing, and capable of endless modifications and delicate shades of expression. Both as a composer and performer his only thought was to embody his own feelings, and that for his own enjoyment. His eye sought no other eye. His execution flowed clear and limpid. His fingers glided over the keys, and the sounds they awoke seemed to follow them like a foaming wave-crest.

But Field won lasting fame less as an exceptionally gifted virtuoso than as an original composer, forming the link in the history of pianoforte-playing between Clementi (in his later period) and Chopin. Though all the rest of his piano works should be forgotten, as most of them are already, his memory is fragrantly and lastingly embalmed in his Nocturnes. Not only the name but also the whole style and matter of these pieces, were strikingly new and original. Up to his time a composition had as a matter of course to be written in the form of a sonata, a rondo, or something of the sort. Field was the first to introduce a style in no way derived from the established categories, and in which feeling and melody, freed from the trammels of coercive form, reign supreme. He opened the way for all the productions which have since appeared under the various titles of Songs without Words, Impromptus, Ballades, etc., and to him we may trace the origin of pieces designed to portray subjective and profound emotion. To these nocturnes ("night-pieces"), so aptly named by their author, Chopin and the pianists following him owe—more or less directly—much of their inspiration. And from them the inspired interpreter and wrapt listener will be able to learn far more of Field's true soul-life than can be taught by a few lines of plain prose. THEO. BAKER.

ON JOHN FIELD'S NOCTURNES*

BY

FRANZ LISZT

THE publication of the first six Nocturnes by Field, united here for the first time, will assuredly meet the desires of all who feel the poignant charm of these tender poems. Hitherto one had to seek them in various editions, the author having carelessly strewn them along his path ; for he showed the same negligence in their publication as in their performance—a negligence which enhanced the grace of his talent, but which causes his admirers regret at the difficulty of collecting his compositions, genuine masterpieces of refined emotion. It is a pity that rights of proprietorship still prevent the issue of a complete edition ; a collection has been made, at least, of those numbers the reprinting of which was authorized.

Field's Nocturnes have preserved their youth beside so many works untimely aged ! After more than thirty-six years they still retain a balmy freshness, and seem to exhale copious perfumes. Where else shall we meet such a perfection of incomparable *naiveté ?* No one since then has been able to reproduce the charms of his speech, caressful as a moist and tender gaze ; soothing as the slow, measured rocking of a boat or the swinging of a hammock, amid whose smoothly placid oscillations we seem to hear the dying murmur of melting caresses. No one has revived these vague Æolian tones, these half-sighs of the breezes, plaintive wailings, ecstatic moanings. No one has dared attempt them ; no one, especially, who had heard Field himself play, or rather dream, his pieces, wrapt in inspiration, not limiting himself to the written notes, but incessantly inventing new groups wherewith to engarland his melodies ; at each repetition he would adorn them diversely with a flowery rain, yet they never wholly disappeared beneath an ornamentation which veiled, without hiding, their languishing undulations and ravishing outlines. What an inexhaustible wealth of variations did he lavish on the embellishment of his thought ! With what rare taste would he intertwine around it, without smothering it, the most subtle weft of arabesques !

Having once surrendered oneself to the placid emotion which sways his compositions, as it swayed his playing, one cannot avoid the conviction that it would be quite useless to attempt to copy him, or to hope happily to imitate this delicate originality, which excluded neither extreme simplicity of sentiment, nor variety of form and embellishment. If there be anything whereof one vainly tries to discover the secret, when Nature has not dowered us therewith, and thus set her seal on our talent, it is the grace of frankness and the charm of ingenuousness. One may possess them as an innate gift, but they cannot be acquired. Field had this gift, and thereby his compositions will ever retain an attraction, over which time has no power. His form will not grow old, because it is perfectly adapted to his conceptions, which do not belong to a class of temporary, transient sentiments, called into being by the influence of his environment at the time, but are pure emotions which will for ever cast their spell over the heart of man ; for he finds them always the same, whether contrasted with the beauties of Nature or with the fondest happiness revealed to him at the morn of life, before the radiant prisms of emotion are overclouded by the shadow of reflection. One may, therefore, not even dream of forming oneself upon this admirable model, because one cannot attain, without unique aspiration, to those effects which are found only when unsought. To analyze the charm of their spontaneity would be a vain task. They emanate solely from a temperament like that of Field. For him, invention and facility were one, diversity of form a necessity, as is usually the case with those who are filled to overflowing with an emotion. Therefore, despite this elegance, which varied so greatly with his moods, there was no trace of affectation in his talent ; far from this, his exquisiteness had all the simplicity of instinct, which delights in endless modulation of the simple and happy chord of the sentiment with which the heart is filled.

And what we say is equally applicable to the composer and the virtuoso. Both in writing and in playing, his sole idea was fully to express his own conceptions to himself ; one cannot imagine a franker disregard of the public than was his. When he came to Paris, he did not refuse to play on square pianos at his concerts, though their effect was certainly not equal to that which he might have obtained on an instrument better suited to the halls in which he gathered attentive audiences, holding them spellbound without himself being aware of it. His almost immovable attitude and but slightly expressive face attracted no attention. His eye sought no other eye. His execution flowed

---

* Written to accompany the first collection of Field's Nocturnes, revised by Liszt, and published by J. Schuberth & Co. at Leipzig in 1859.

clear and limpid. His fingers glided over the keys, and the sounds they awoke seemed to follow them like a foaming wave-crest. It was easy to see, that for him his chief auditor was himself. His tranquillity was wellnigh somnolent, and the impression that might be made on his hearers was his least care. No abruptness, no shock, either in gesture or rhythm, ever supervened to interrupt his melodious revery, whose fondly murmurous melodies, *mezza voce*, spread through the air on delicious waves the most suave impressions. the most charming surprises of the heart !

This calm tranquillity not merely never abandoned him, but seemed, on the contrary, to absorb him more and more. As he grew older, he conceived an antipathy against noise and movement in general. He loved silence ; he spoke softly and slowly. All things brusque and turbulent were repugnant to him, and he fled them. His execution, of such good taste and rare distinction, became impregnated with a morbid languor which appeared to grow more and more indolent. To avoid the least unnecessary agitation, it was his habit to place a large coin on the back of his hand, and to practise his daily exercises, continued into his old age—a custom now, alas, sadly neglected !—with it in that position, never making it fall by a violent gesture. This trait gives a perfect idea of the placidity of his playing and his character. During his last years complete indifference took possession of him, influencing all his personal habits ; to rise, to sit down again, to walk, was fatiguing to him. A light cane was at times too heavy a burden for his indolent hand, and if he let it drop from sheer lack of energy to hold it, he would remain standing beside it until some passer-by picked it up for him.

With regard to his fame, his attitude was quite similar. No care, no anxiety concerning it, occupied him ; he was careless of being widely known, or of having his praises trumpeted abroad. Art consisted, for him, in the satisfaction which he found in giving himself up to it. He cared not at all for the rest, for the place which might be assigned him, for the renown which might surround him, for the success or the life of his works. Field sang to and for himself, and his own enjoyment sufficed him ; he asked nothing more of music. He wrote, as it were, for pastime. Several of his works, the tale of which is far too scanty, and more especially his concertos, contain pages of striking originality, and of incontestable harmonic merit ; but while studying them and becoming permeated with their meaning, one is led to the belief that both in composing and performing them he but sought to satisfy his imaginative faculty—creating without effort, perfecting without trouble, and publishing with indifference. How great the contrast with our present customs !

To this total absence of all seeking after effect, we owe the first—so finished !—essays ventured on the piano by emotion and revery to free themselves from the constraint imposed, by the regular and official mould, on all compositions. Up to his time they had to be sonatas, or rondos, or something of the sort. Field was the first to introduce a style in no way derived from the established categories, and in which feeling and melody, freed from the trammels of coercive form, reign supreme. He opened the way for all the productions which have since appeared under the various titles of Songs without Words, Impromptus, Ballades, etc., and to him we may trace the origin of pieces designed to portray subjective and profound emotion. He it was who discovered this domain, alike so new and so favorable, to imaginations of a subtle rather than grandiose type, to inspirations more tender than lyrical.

The title *Nocturne* aptly applies to the pieces so named by Field, for it bears our thoughts at the outset toward those hours wherein the soul, released from all the cares of day, is lost in self-contemplation, and soars toward the regions of a starlit heaven. We see her hovering on ethereal pinions, like the antique Philomela, over the flowers and perfumes of a nature whereof she is enamoured. The charm, which draws toward these simple and pure impressions the souls which ever retain some youthful instincts, is now doubled by the need of a respite from the forced and unnatural expression of the strongest and most complex passions, as reproduced by a notable contingent of the modern school. Even under the name of Nocturnes, we have seen the shy, serenely tender emotions which Field charged them to interpret, supplanted by strange and foreign effects. Only one genius possessed himself of this style, lending to it all the movement and ardor of which it was susceptible, yet preserving all its tenderness and the poising flight of its aspirations. Filling the entire scope of elegiac sentiment, and coloring his reveries with the profound sadness for which Young found some chords of so dolorous vibration, Chopin, in his poetic Nocturnes, sang not only the harmonies which are the source of our most ineffable delights, but likewise the restless, agitating bewilderment to which they oft give rise. His flight is loftier, though his wing be more wounded ; and his very suaveness grows heartrending, so thinly does it veil his despairful anguish. We may never hope to surpass—which, in the arts, means to equal—that preëminence of inspiration and form wherewith he endowed all the pieces he published under this title. Their closer kinship to sorrow than those of Field renders them the more strongly marked ; their poetry is more sombre and fascinating ; they ravish us more, but are less reposeful ; and thus permit us to return with pleasure to those pearly shells that open, far from the tempests and the immensities of Ocean, beside some murmuring spring shaded by the palms of a happy oasis which makes us forget even the existence of the desert.

The charm which I have always found in these pieces, with their wealth of melody and refinement of harmony, goes back to the years of my earliest childhood. Long before I dreamed of ever meeting their author, I had given myself up for hours at a time to the soothing influences of the visions flowing from the gentle intoxication of this music, comparable to the odorous smoke-wreaths of rose-tobacco substituted, in a narghileh, for the acrid whiffs of *tombeki*—hallucinations free from fever and violent emotion, but filled, on the contrary, with floating iridescent images whose touching beauties, in some moments of happy illusion, reach the intensity of passion. All the emotions that moved to the writing and reading of Idylls and Eclogues are found here in their most charming manifestations. How many moments have I passed while allowing my imagination and my eyes to stray around the name of Mme. de Rosenkampf, to whom the longest and loveliest of these pieces (the Fourth Nocturne) is dedicated! What confused and amiable ideas did I connect with this "Battle of Roses," whence had sprung this inspiration so profoundly felt, so tenderly melancholy, and so felicitous! In it distinction of style rivals grace of sentiment, and it is instinct with so rare a delicacy of ornamentation, and so exquisite an art in the modulation of the thought, that it seems as if the composer could find nothing noble, nothing choice, nothing irreproachable enough while writing these chaste lines.

The first and fifth Nocturnes in this collection are marked by a radiant happiness, one might say an overflowing felicity, evoked without exertion, and enjoyed with pure delight. In the second the tints are darker, like those of daylight in a shady avenue. One might imagine this song imbued with that feeling of absence, of which the poet says: "l'absence est un monde sans soleil." The third and sixth Nocturnes bear a pastoral character; their melodies seem as woven of the balmiest breezes, sighing warmly and moistly; they appear to reflect the changing shades that dye the vapors of dawn, rose tints giving way to bluish, and these in turn to lilac. In the latter, however, the forms stand out more clearly, with sharper outlines, as if oppressive heat had already dissipated the mists of morning. One meets therein with sinuosities like those of a great wave bearing sparkling wavelets resembling diamond chips, rolling its serpentine swells across a landscape radiant with light and freshness. This refulgent clarity offers no dissonant contrast to the titles of these pieces; it was not merely a craving for oddity that caused Field to give the title "Noonday" to a Nocturne which could not be included here. Are not his Nocturnes half-waking dreams, in a night without gloom, like the summer nights in St. Petersburg, whose return he so often saw?—nights in a drapery of white veils that hide nothing from the eye, but only cover all objects with a light mist, like the dull white of a silver crape. A secret harmony dispels the apparent disparity between nocturnal shades and the clear brilliancy of day; and we experience no surprise, so fully does the vagueness of the images let us feel, that they live and move only in the dreamy imagination of the poet, and not in waking reality.

It might be said that Field's entire life, exempt from that overwrought activity which forces on the generality of mankind the desire to strive for the light, and to live in broad daylight,— exempt, as well, from the burning rays projected by vivid passions, and flowing on in dreamy idleness, all in half-tints and *chiaro oscuro*,—itself developed like a long Nocturne, without the lightning of any storm, and wherein no blustering tempest ever marred the calm of reposeful nature. Born in Dublin, Ireland, in 1782, and for years a resident of London, he left that city while yet a youth as the attached companion of his master, Clementi, whom he followed to Paris, Germany, and Russia, settling in St. Petersburg. Here, and in Moscow, his lessons were eagerly sought, and estimated at their full value; during many years his time was in such eager request, that he sometimes heard, while still lying in bed in the morning, his pupils playing in an adjoining room. Towards the end of his career, perchance drawn by some mirage of his fancy, he set out to visit Italy; passing through Paris, where, despite growing weakness, he gave concerts, and proceeding to Naples. But these too brilliant skies, and the climate, did not agree with him. He fell ill, and returned to Russia in 1835, where he was received with the same warmhearted benevolence which had always been extended to him in this, his second fatherland, which adopted him so truly that he was almost made a national celebrity. Here he ended his life in 1837.

A favorite pupil of Clementi, he learned from this great master the secrets of the finest execution known at that period, and employed it in a style of poetry wherein he will ever be an incomparable model of grace unconscious of itself, of melancholy artlessness, of refinement and natural ease alike. He is one of those types of a primitive school, with which one meets only at certain artistic epochs, when art, beginning to divine her resources, has not yet exhausted them so far as to venture to extend her domain, in order to develop her powers more freely, even at the risk of breaking her wings more than once while essaying to cast off her trammels.

(Translated by Th. Baker.)

Thematic Index.

Nocturne Pastorale.

Nocturne caractéristique.
"NOONTIDE."

Rêverie - Nocturne.

Cradle Song.

Song without Words.

Nocturne.

I.

JOHN FIELD.

Molto moderato.

Piano.

mezza voce

Printed in the U. S. A.

4

Nocturne.
II.

Moderato e molto espressivo.

JOHN FIELD.

Piano.

Nocturne.
III.

Un poco allegretto.

JOHN FIELD.

Piano.

Nocturne.
IV.

JOHN FIELD.

Poco Adagio.

Ped. at each quarter beat.

Nocturne

John Field

Nocturne.
Cradle-Song.
VI.

JOHN FIELD.

Andante tranquillo

Piano.

Nocturne.
VII.

JOHN FIELD.

Andante.

Piano.

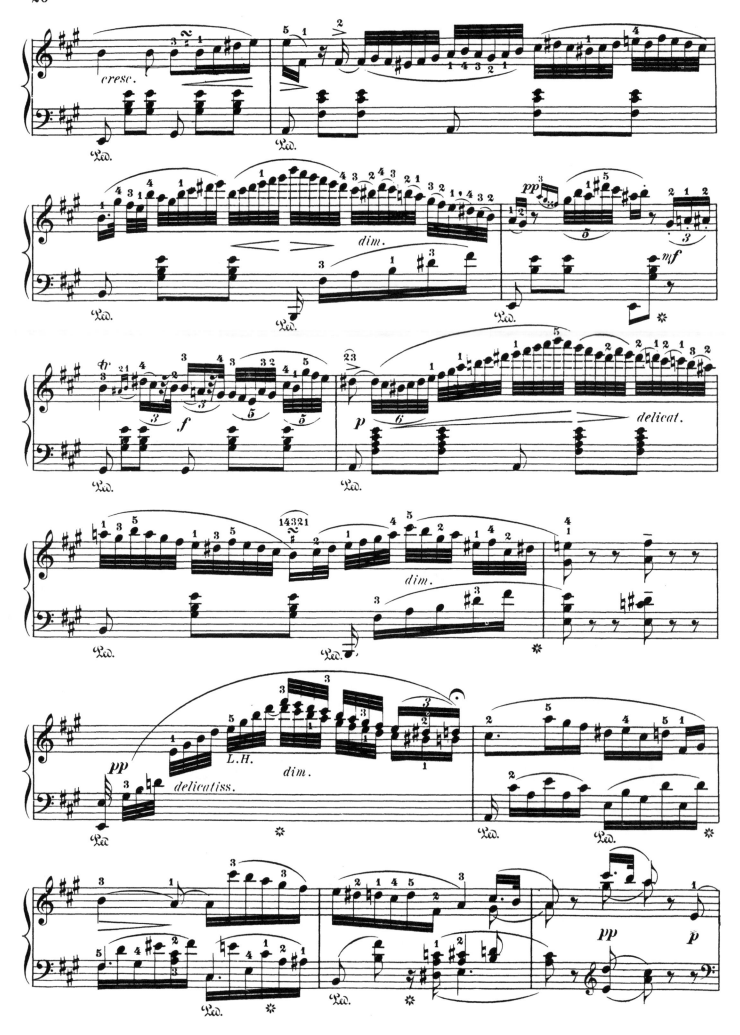

Nocturne.

VIII.

JOHN FIELD

Andante spianato.

Piano.

Nocturne.
IX.

JOHN FIELD.

Nocturne Pastorale.

X.

Andante con moto.

JOHN FIELD.

Nocturne.

XI.

Edited and revised by
E. TAUSIG.

JOHN FIELD.

Moderato. (♩.= 100.)

Piano.

Nocturne Caractéristique.

"Noontide."

In Rondo Form.

JOHN FIELD

Rêverie-Nocturne.

XIII.

JOHN FIELD.

Sognante. ($\quarternote$ = 76)

Piano.

Nocturne.

XIV.

Lento. (♪ = 108)

JOHN FIELD.

Piano.

Nocturne
(Song without Words)

JOHN FIELD

Nocturne

XVI.

JOHN FIELD.

Molto moderato. ($\bullet$ = 88)

Piano.

Nocturne.

XVII.

Molto moderato. (♩ = 80.)

JOHN FIELD.

Piano

Nocturne.

XVIII.

JOHN FIELD.